Original title:
Whale Songs in the Ocean's Silence

Copyright © 2025 Creative Arts Management OÜ
All rights reserved.

Author: Riley Hawthorne
ISBN HARDBACK: 978-1-80587-463-8
ISBN PAPERBACK: 978-1-80587-933-6

Invoices of the Underwater Realm

In the depths where fish do thrive,
Octopus, with ink, tries to connive.
Claiming he did paint the sea,
But all he drew was a jelly spree.

He sends a bill for kelp and foam,
A contract sealed in conch-shell dome.
But every fin and tail just laugh,
At the artist's fluid path and gaffe.

Serene Songs of the Midnight Sea

The fish gather 'round for open mic,
Under the moon, they dance and hike.
A clam croons out a soothing tune,
While crabs tap-dance beneath the moon.

Inky squids, flavors bold and bright,
Beatbox with bubbles, a comical sight.
The starfish clap with all their might,
As dolphins giggle in pure delight.

The Solitude of Oceanic Voices

Deep down below, where the silence drapes,
A turtle complains of tangled tape.
'I've lost my way,' he grumbles loud,
'Next time, I'll follow the fishy crowd!'

With echoes of laughter in the blue,
The plankton can never keep their view.
They swirl and twirl in jumbled glee,
Making a mess like lost debris.

An Underwater Ballad of the Ancients

The ancients tell tales of bubbles and spits,
Where fish share gossip, and laughter splits.
A whale in the corner, with a spoon for a hat,
Claims he once tangoed with a rather large cat.

He spins grand stories, covering whales,
Of seaweed picnics and shimmery trails.
The sea anemones sway to the beat,
As they dance in their homes, so soft and sweet.

The Call of the Vast Expanse

In the depths where the fishes play,
A big fellow hums, not a word to say.
Blowholes puffing, a grand serenade,
Making waves like a musical parade.

Bubbles burst with each laugh they send,
Giggling echoes, a finned friend.
Swishing tails make a splashy beat,
Dancing kelp twirls, it's quite the feat!

Rhythms of the Celestial Sea

Around the reef, a waltz begins,
Fins flapping lightly, oh let's dive in!
A sea turtle tumbles, a clown in disguise,
With a wiggle and giggle, it steals the prize.

Fish in the colors of a paintbox bright,
Twist and twirl in the shimmering light.
Jellyfish jiggle, they bobble and sway,
In this underwater cabaret, hip-hip-hooray!

Secrets in the Soundless Depths

In midnight blue where shadows creep,
A narwhal croons, making creatures leap.
With a honk that echoes, it's quite the show,
Even the octopus joins in the flow!

What mysteries hide in the silent void?
Fishy gossip keeps everyone buoyed.
A crab with a microphone, all ears are near,
As they share silly tales that bring hearty cheer!

An Ocean's Whisper

Beneath the waves, the whispers rise,
A playful dolphin with mischief in its eyes.
"Let's prank the squids!" it joyfully yells,
As they twirl in circles and swim in swells.

A clumsy snapper trips on a shell,
Laughing so hard, it can't quite tell.
And with each splash, they dance and tease,
An ocean of giggles, quite sure to please!

The Quiet Symphony of the Seas

Bubbles burst like giggles
As fish dance in their suits.
A clam's got quite the wiggle,
But always missing boots!

Octopus plays the tuba,
While the seaweed offers snacks.
A crab with charm and makeup,
Is pulling in the quacks!

The starfish clap their tiny hands,
To the beat of jelly sways.
Marine life makes wild plans,
For lazy, silly days!

With sea foam as confetti,
And oysters joining in,
The ocean's perfect petty,
When laughter has to win!

Echoing Murmurs from Below

Beneath the waves, a chatter,
A lobster tells a joke.
A dolphin's laughter splatters,
With every little poke.

Puffers puff up with laughter,
As eels wiggle with glee.
A tricky game, thereafter,
Of hide and seek at sea!

The bubbles form a mob,
Laughing as they float away.
The ocean's wondrous job,
Is keeping blues at bay!

A whale hums a silly tune,
While clowns of anemones,
Dance beneath the silver moon,
In comical, wavy knees!

Tales Carried by the Current

Once a fish with a hat,
Claimed the sea was his home.
He laughed and patted a scat,
Wishing for some foamy foam.

Jellyfish wrote memoirs,
Of their stings and dance fights.
Sea turtles tell tales of cars,
While trying to catch the lights!

The currents swirl their stories,
Of barnacles with charm.
Nudibranchs bask in glories,
Wearing colors that disarm!

Coral reefs clap in delight,
As planktons spin their yarns.
Every day feels so right,
In the ocean's humorous charms!

Nocturnal Choirs of the Deep

At night the sea starts to chuckle,
With creatures dressed in dreams.
A fish hums with all its muscle,
As moonlight softly beams.

An owl fish plays the castanet,
While squids juggle seaweed.
There's never a chance to fret,
Where laughter plants a seed!

The crabs perform in mimes,
Dancing under soft blue lights.
Their rhythm plays with the tides,
In these wacky, deep delights!

From plankton tunes to whale beats,
The giggles rise and flow.
In the dark where humor greets,
The ocean's nighttime show!

Chords Above the Ocean Floor

Beneath the waves, a tickle and a tease,
Blubbery ballads float with effortless ease.
Fish gather 'round for a grand old show,
Shake your fins, it's time to go!

A trumpet here, a bubble there,
Sea critters dancing with flair everywhere.
The octopus joins in, not shy at all,
With eight arms waving, he takes his call!

An Ode to the Untold Depths

In the deep blue, where jesters play,
Gurgling giggles greet each new day.
Crabs crawling in a conga line,
Wiggle your tentacles as you dine!

Eels in tuxedos, feeling quite grand,
Swirling around like they're in a band.
A dolphin with glasses snaps a photo,
While all the mermaids yell, "Go, Toto!"

Songsters of the Briny Deep

Bubbles rise up like giggles in pairs,
Melodies drift through seaweed's flares.
Clams clap their shells with impeccable cheer,
Their rhythm is funky, let's spread it here!

Guitarfish strum on the coral's edge,
With sea cucumbers forming a pledge.
To keep the humor flowing all night,
Puffers puff up and take flight!

Serenades in the Swells

In the swells, where the currents collide,
Laughter echoes as fish slip and glide.
The porpoises prank with a splashy delight,
Their jokes make the starfish roll in the light!

A sea sponge hums a whimsical tune,
While jellyfish jig and sway in the moon.
Whimsical wonders in waters so bright,
Join in, dear friends, it's a slippery night!

Echoes of the Deep Blue

In the depths where fish do play,
Bubbles burst and drift away.
A trumpetfish holds quite a tune,
While jellyfish dance to a silent moon.

Clownfish giggle as they swim,
Tickling seaweed on a whim.
A grumpy shark shakes his head,
Wishing for a bed instead.

Starfish claps with arms so wide,
As an octopus joins in the ride.
They skip along the sandy floor,
Who knew they could dance and more?

A crab says, "Hey, let's throw a bash!"
"I'll serve up seaweed with a splash!"
And just like that, the deep goes wild,
A carnival with striped fish beguiled.

Serenade of the Blue Giants

Gigantic creatures swim and sway,
With laughter bubbling, they splay.
The bass turns up, the krill take flight,
As they groove beneath day and night.

A bluefin tuna wears a hat,
He says, "Join me, my dear cat!"
While dolphins flip in sheer delight,
Chasing seaweed with all their might.

"Do the cha-cha," says the seal,
As seagulls dance on a spinning reel.
The ocean floor a dance hall bright,
Where every fish ignites the night.

A beluga winks with glee,
"Let's make a splash, come swim with me!"
They twirl and whirl in frothy play,
As currents giggle and sway.

Melodies Beneath the Waves

Notes float gently from below,
Anemones sway to the flow.
Eels do disco in the sand,
With sea cucumbers lending a hand.

A shrimp takes center stage and grins,
While turtles bop to seaweed spins.
Clams clap shells, keeping time,
A conch joins in, feeling sublime.

Sardines swirl in a shimmering ball,
While krill form lines, one and all.
"Hey, don't forget the shrimp charade!"
"Shall we dance till the sun does fade?"

From gobies to crabs, the floor's alive,
In the underwater jive, they thrive.
With bubbles popping and laughter wide,
Ocean's party, no need to hide.

Sonic Whispers of the Abyss

Down below where the shadows creep,
Creatures gather in a playful heap.
"Pass the plankton!" calls a clown,
As bubbles rise and settle down.

A narwhal blows a silly tune,
While swimming by a tattered balloon.
"Let's throw a party in this depth!"
With friendly fish, no secrets kept!

A flounder flops in with a grin,
"Who wore it better? The sea or fin?"
Crabs debate over sea-style chic,
While wrasses tease with playful sneak.

With laughter echoing from the floor,
The deep has never seen this more.
From starry eyes to happy shrieks,
The ocean sings for fun, unique!

Celestial Whispers Beneath the Waves

In the deep, fish dance and sway,
While a crab tries to join the ballet.
He twirls with flair, but oh dear me,
He trips on a shell, not so fancy-free!

The octopus plays with its ink,
Drawing pictures that make one think.
A dolphin giggles with a flip,
While a starfish just gives a wink and a skip!

Turtles playing tag with a fish,
Who insists they can grant any wish.
But the fish just keeps swimming in circles,
While the turtles ponder their deeds as mere sparkles!

So beneath the waves, what a sight,
Creatures having a laugh, pure delight.
In a world of bubbles and scaling blues,
Misadventures play out, like silly news!

The Ocean's Songs of Solace

There's a seahorse with a cowboy hat,
Riding the currents, oh how he'd prat!
He toots his trumpet, makes the waves clap,
All while avoiding an armchair map!

A jellyfish juggles blue glowing lights,
As an eel breaks out in electric fights.
Clownfish crack jokes, they really can chat,
While the hermit crab hides, he's too shy for that!

The starry sky can't compete with this crew,
As bubbles burst tell tales that are true.
Corals crease with laughter, a colorful scene,
While fish throw confetti, it's all quite serene!

So down in the depths, where silliness swells,
Creatures spin tales like eavesdropping spells.
With laughter and glee, they sway through the blue,
The ocean's own symphony, funny and true!

Murmurs of the Hidden Current

Imagine a squid with a penchant for rhyme,
Spinning a tale, oh it takes its time!
With ink pots alight, it writes in the sea,
Of crabby warriors and turtles with glee!

Fish in a choir sing off-key,
As a dolphin sneezes, saying "Excuse me!"
Echoes of laughter ripple like waves,
In this comedy deep, everyone behaves!

A porcupine puffer gets stuck in a net,
Turns into a balloon, can you imagine the threat?
With a pop and a splash, he floats to the air,
Murmurs of giggles, nobody a care!

So swirl in the currents, find fun like gold,
Beneath the blue where adventures unfold.
In ridiculous tales so wonderfully absurd,
The deep sea delight is a treasure unheard!

The Choir of Silent Giants

In the depths where the giants roam,
They practice scales from their ocean home.
With a splash and a giggle, they sing,
Making waves while they jive and swing.

Their music drifts through the dark blue sea,
Fishes dance, joining in with glee.
A bass so deep it shakes the ground,
While crabs tap their claws to the sound.

Bubbles pop in a rhythmic beat,
As sea urchins sway on their tiny feet.
A kelp forest sways in the breeze,
Grooving along with the ocean's tease.

With a beluga's wink and a dolphin's spin,
They harmonize, let the fun begin!
Who knew that giggles could echo so wide?
In the funhouse of waves, they take great pride.

Symphony of the Endless Deep

Down where the currents twist and swirl,
An orchestra plays with a flip and a whirl.
Turtles conduct with a flippered sway,
While jellyfish float and drift away.

The clownfish jest in a colorful show,
Tickling anemones, making them glow.
Octopuses juggle with eight funny arms,
Creating a spectacle with their charming charms.

Tangled in kelp, a group starts to hum,
Even the sea cucumbers can't resist the fun.
With glances and giggles, they share a big grin,
As the music of laughter echoes from fin.

In the quiet of blue, a party unfolds,
Where even the shyest of fish break their molds.
So here's to the depths, where silly meets sweet,
In the symphony grand, life's a hilarious treat!

Echoes in the Liquid Horizon

Bubbles burst with a fizzy delight,
In the great depths where creatures take flight.
A squawk from a parrotfish, what a surprise!
While the sea stars giggle with wide-open eyes.

The seaweed sways, caught in the groove,
As playful dolphins begin to move.
With flips and twists, they dance with ease,
Creating a ruckus that echoes through seas.

Grouchy old crabs join in the play,
Grabbing their shells, trying to sway.
But every attempt to find their groove,
Ends up in laughter, oh what a move!

So sing with the currents, let folly reign,
In the deep blue, joy is never plain.
For even the shyest fish can't help but laugh,
In the endless waves, they find their own path.

Ballads of the Forgotten Depths

In waters deep where secrets lie,
The fish share tales with a wink and a sigh.
Old shipwrecks tell stories of treasure and fun,
While the sea cucumbers chuckle, "Oh, what a run!"

Slugs in hats and snails on parade,
Conducting grand shows, they're never afraid.
With tap-dancing flounders leading the way,
They create a commotion, come join the fray!

As eels sneak peeks with electric grins,
The laughter rolls out as the fun begins.
Even the hermit crabs nod to the beat,
Snapping their claws in a rhythmic retreat.

So let the depths be a haven for jest,
Where silliness reigns and laughter's the quest.
In the ballads sung from the ocean's heart,
Every creature finds joy, each playing their part.

The Language of the Liquid Sky

In the deep, the bubbles rise,
Fish converse with silly sighs.
A squid in a tux, oh what a sight,
Dancing under the moonlight.

Starfish gossip, tales absurd,
Jellyfish giggle, wobbly words.
Crabs recite their crabby jokes,
Tickling the seaweed, laughing folks.

Sea cucumbers in a debate,
Claiming they're the ocean's fate.
But who would trust a veggie friend,
When the fish fry and diver dive blend?

In currents strong, they lose their flow,
Their punchlines drift, just where'd they go?
Yet in the splash, laughter we find,
A symphony of sea life, never confined.

Celestial Notes of the Deep

A dolphin's whistle, such a tease,
Tickling the whale, as it sneezes.
Stars peek in, they're quite amused,
As the kelp just shakes, so confused.

Guitar fish strum with their tails,
While mackerel sing funny tales.
Octopuses play the accordion,
Their eight arms dance like a champion.

From coral reefs, the laughter flows,
Critters share gossip nobody knows.
A crab with a monocle sips champagne,
Declaring himself the ocean's brain.

Bubbles burst with giggles galore,
Who knew the ocean could entertain more?
In every current, humor hides,
With every wave, a new joke glides.

Dreams of Melodic Currents

Fish wear hats as they swim in schools,
Debating who's the best at tools.
Anemones wiggle in a flow of glee,
While a clam keeps time with a raucous plea.

A grouper dreams of Broadway fame,
Practicing lines with a goofy name.
Shrimps critique his big debut,
With popcorn snacks and seaweed stew.

Manta rays glide with a flair of grace,
But lose the beat in an awkward chase.
Their clumsy moves make all seas sigh,
As they trip the light fantastic in the tide.

With a splash and a giggle, they sway and twirl,
An undersea dance, a watery whirl.
In dreams of currents, laughter's theme,
The creatures chuckle at their own meme.

Resonance of Forgotten Giants

In the depths, there's a jolly old giant,
With a belly full of fish, quite defiant.
He hums a tune that shakes the sea,
    Causing each little fish to flee.

Turtles wear shades, looking quite sly,
    Chasing bubbles that float on by.
They chuckle at a snail's slow pace,
Challenging him to a racing space.

Anglerfish flash their quirky grin,
Reeling in jokes like they're all in.
Their light so bright, they steal the show,
    As they tell fishy tales, fast or slow.

So here's to the giants, old yet spry,
With laughter and music, they soar in the sky.
Beneath the waves, joy springs unfurled,
    In the heart of the ocean, a funny world.

Lament of the Ocean's Keepers

Bubbles rise with a giggly cheer,
Fish dance about, spreading silly fear.
Seagulls squawk with an awkward grace,
Crabs sidestep in a comical race.

Turtles ponder their rock-paper-scissors,
While dolphins joke, tossing slippery blizzards.
Octopuses plan their prank-filled schemes,
Flipping their arms like aquatic dreams.

Jellyfish wiggling, with jiggly bellies,
Whispering tales of their oozy jellies.
Clownfish laughing, in colors so bright,
Tickling each other, what a funny sight!

Stars twinkle down on the joyous sea,
As every creature sings, "Join the spree!"
With bubbles of laughter, they float around,
In this watery world, silliness is found.

The Harmonic Tide of Nature

The ocean waves have so much to say,
Ticklish crabs dance in their own ballet.
Shells clack together, a musical mime,
While fish make splashy beats all the time.

A turtle yodels with joy and flair,
The seaweed sways like it just doesn't care.
Flounders float in a comical haze,
Caught in a dance, lost in their daze.

Barnacles chant with a crusty tune,
Under the gaze of the bright, silly moon.
With a wink and a wiggle, they sing along,
In the grand underwater, harmonious throng.

Laughter bounces off bubbles so light,
As sea creatures joke in the shimmering night.
This silly symphony, a splashy delight,
Conducted by nature, what a grand sight!

Echoing Through Aquatic Realms

Voices echo with splashes and giggles,
As fish tell tales that make everyone wiggle.
Seahorses prance in a comical ball,
They twirl and spin, trying not to fall.

Mollusks drum on their shells with a beat,
Conch shells echo, "Can you feel the heat?"
Anemones bounce, their tentacles sway,
Inviting all creatures to join in play.

With bubbles and giggles, the orchestra grows,
A silly parade where the weirdness flows.
Sharks tell jokes, with bewildering grins,
As eels wrap around, giving them spins.

Under this dome of blue with bright light,
Silly serenades fill up the night.
Nature's echoing laughter rings true,
In the depths of the ocean, awaits a zoo!

The Melodic Pulse of the Sea

In the ocean's heart, a rhythm takes flight,
Fish join the band with scales shining bright.
Grouchy old clams clack in their shell,
Creating a melody, a hilarious spell.

Frolicking dolphins, they leap and they dive,
Making tunes that make the sea come alive.
Starfish play maracas; they rattle away,
On this funny stage where sea life loves to play.

Kraken croons softly, its voice full of sass,
As colorful parrotfish shimmy and pass.
The coral reefs sway, a colorful scene,
With all of the laughter, it's a comic routine.

So dive into laughter; let the waves guide,
In this oceanic concert, no need to hide.
With every splash and every chime,
The sea's pulse beats, dancing in time.

The Soundtrack of the Sea's Embrace

In the deep, a croaky cheer,
Fish dance close, swapping a sneer.
Octopus plays the sax with flair,
Crabs tap feet without a care.

Turtles hum a tuneful blend,
While seaweed sways like it's on trend.
Clams chime in with a clang and clatter,
Bright bubbles form, oh, what a chatter!

Timeless Currents of Melody

Bubbles pop, like jokes in air,
A dolphin giggles, full of flair.
The starfish tries a little jig,
But trips over a seaweed twig!

The anemone hosts a band,
With squishy friends, they take a stand.
They sing of picnic plans so bold,
While sea turtles munch on mold!

Murmurs from the Blue Depths

Echoes bounce with playful glee,
A seahorse gallops, let it be!
Jellyfish glow, like lights so bright,
Making waves to dance at night.

Pufferfish puff with a plucky grin,
"I'll roll the beats, let's begin!"
With a splash and a wink, they play all day,
In the ocean's light-hearted ballet.

Chorus of the Abyssal Realm

Hoots and honks, a silly show,
A crab with glasses steals the glow.
The sea cucumbers sing a tune,
As fish wear hats and shout, "We're a croon!"

A whale in shades swims by with style,
"Join the chorus, stay awhile!"
Flippers wave, the currents sway,
In this joyful ocean ballet!

Cascading Voices of the Depths

Bubbles rise and giggles drift,
Fish in tuxedos dance and shift.
Turtles hum a merry tune,
While crabs play cards with a silver spoon.

Starfish cheer in their own way,
Making waves on a lazy day.
Seahorses prance, what a sight!
Even the squids join in for a night.

The deep blue laughs, oh what a tease,
Sea cucumbers rolling with ease.
Clownfish joke and tickle a mate,
As cookie-cutter sharks just contemplate.

From coral castles to seaweed fields,
All share the laughter that the ocean yields.
Manta rays glide with slick moves,
In this party, everyone grooves.

Songs of the Sunken Giants

In the wreck of a ship, a clam plays the flute,
While a herring struts in a shiny suit.
Octopuses juggle shells with glee,
Singing happily, "Come join me!"

Giant squids drape themselves on a throne,
Pretending to be kings all alone.
With a wink and a wave, they make their decree,
"Hands off our treasure, it's got legs and a knee!"

Eels twist and shout, a slippery lot,
In a conga line, they dance on the spot.
And down in the deep where it often turns dark,
The anglerfish laughs, "I've got the best spark!"

These behemoths of waters, bold and bright,
Chuckle together through day and night.
With laughter that echoes in currents so grand,
Who knew the ocean could be so unplanned?

A Lullaby for the Sea's Spirits

The waves hum a tune, soft and sweet,
Beneath the moon, where the fishes meet.
Jellyfish sway in pajamas of light,
Singing softly to coax the night.

Driftwood whispers tales of jest,
While barnacles snore, taking a rest.
Clownfish giggle at a passing shark,
"Can't catch me, I'm too quick for the dark!"

A gentle breeze tickles the sand,
Sea otters toss shells, so they planned.
The ocean's lullaby drifts far and wide,
In this underwater world, we take great pride.

With bubbles that pop and seagrass that sways,
The creatures of night are here to play.
So close your eyes, let the sea serenade,
Tomorrow we'll dance, in watery parade!

Secret Melodies of Undersea Valleys

In valleys deep where secrets lie,
Sea urchins whistle, oh my, oh my!
Blowfish puff out with a cheeky grin,
Making friends with the guppies within.

Caves echo laughter from fishes galore,
They challenge the tides for a fun ocean tour.
"Catch me if you can!" shouts a vibrant clown,
As he twirls his way through the seaweed town.

Lobsters snicker at their treasure maps,
While shrimp throw parties, handing out snacks.
The narwhals compete, a quirky parade,
"It's my turn now," one narwhal displayed!

With bubbles and giggles, the valleys resound,
In this underwater realm, joys abound.
So dive right in, you'll find your delight,
Where the sea creatures play from morning till night!

Cadence of the Marine Night

Under the stars, fish dance around,
They twirl so fast, they can't hear a sound.
A crab in pajamas, lost in its dream,
Singing to turtles like it's a meme.

Jellyfish jive in a glowing parade,
Bubbles pop laughter, the ocean's charade.
Starfish are chatting, their jokes are quite strange,
While dolphins are rolling, performing a range.

Seahorses giggle, they wear tiny hats,
And octopuses juggle blue rubber mats.
The rhythm of waves keeps the misplaced beat,
As fish tell the tale of the knight and his fleet.

So let's dive below, where mischief must brew,
In the kingdom of glee, where silliness grew.
For every wave whispers a joke just for you,
In the cadence of night, oh what a view!

Waves of Solitude and Song

A lonely clam hums a soft, silly tune,
While squids paint the sea in the light of the moon.
Their inks create pictures that swirl all about,
As fish form a conga line, giggling and stout.

The seaweed sways with a flowery flair,
As plankton play hide and seek, oh what a scare!
The echoes of laughter stitch tales in the tide,
While shells crack up, though they try to hide.

A dolphin is rapping with rhythm and cheer,
While sharks throw a party, pouring out beer.
Starfish try to tango but trip on the sand,
With jellyfish hosting, it's quite unplanned.

So heed the ocean's whimsy, rise and dive,
For the waves share giggles that help you survive.
Among bubbling blues, nonsense is king,
In a world where the tides dance and sing!

The Deep's Hidden Harmonies

Bubbles float up while a pufferfish grins,
Singing the lyrics in undersea bins.
A snail plays a harp made of seaweed and slime,
And crabs pull a prank, saying, "It's time!"

The bottom is knitted with laughter and glee,
As clams hold a concert, all under the sea.
A clam is a diva, a fish plays guitar,
And seahorses dream of being superstar.

Anemones giggle, they tickle the reef,
While barnacles boast about their grand chief.
A sea lion juggles some floating kelp rings,
In harmony's depths, everybody sings.

So come join the madness, swim down for a while,
In the deep's silly ways, with a splash and a smile.
For in every corner, a chuckle awaits,
As laughter spreads wide, just like tidal fates!

Echoes of Celestial Waters

Fish tell tall tales of a ship made of cheese,
Where mermaids serve crackers, they aim to please.
The octopus hears, with a nod and a grin,
While his eight arms juggle, it's where fun begins.

A shrimp runs a marathon, swift as a flash,
As dolphins just giggle, they cheer with a splash.
Turtles in bow ties sing tunes from the past,
In this sanctuary, where silliness lasts.

Skates glide on glitter, while lanternfish hum,
Telling the big waves to quiet their drum.
The chorus of clowns, all swimming around,
Crafting a symphony that tickles the sound.

So venture beneath where the humor unfolds,
In the echoes of waters, a story is told.
With each little ripple, a chuckle we find,
In the deep's playful heart, oh, joy intertwined!

An Ocean's Heartfelt Serenade

Bubbles rise as laughter floats,
Fish dance like they're on boats.
Splashing tunes, a wavy beat,
In this sea, we all have feet.

Crabs join in with tiny claps,
Seagulls flap and give their laughs.
Starfish play the ukulele,
Jellyfish are quite silly, maybe!

Turtles spin like disco queens,
While octopuses strum their dreams.
In this ocean, joy is bright,
A party where we sing at night.

So grab your fins and join the scene,
In watery fun, we reign supreme!
With every splash, a giggle grows,
An ocean's heart forever glows.

Melodies Wrapped in Liquid Dreams

In water's depths, a chorus swells,
Gurgling giggles, happy yells.
Seahorses prance in grand ballet,
While dolphins make jokes all day.

Clownfish wear the funniest hats,
While lounging next to sleeping cats.
A crab plays piano on a shell,
Everything's cozy; all is well.

Bubble trails are like sweet tunes,
Waltzing 'neath the laughing moons.
Eels sneak up with a funny dance,
Creating waves of humor's chance!

So if you dive and feel the cheer,
Know fun awaits when you come near!
Liquid laughter fills the air,
An ocean's joy is truly rare.

The Language of Delicate Whispers

In whispered depths, the fish collide,
Talking bubbles, side by side.
A sea cucumber tells a tale,
Of a crab who went to sail.

Waves giggle as they softly break,
The anemone starts to shake.
Starfish share their weirdest dreams,
And seaweed joins in funny schemes.

A porpoise relay, quite the thrill,
With jokes that make the ocean chill.
Tangs swim by with bubble chats,
While all around dance silly spats.

The sea is bright with rhythmic glee,
Where every wave's a melody.
In this world of aquatic fun,
The laughter's just never done!

Rhythmic Echoes of the Deep

Under waves, the rhythms boom,
As fish create their own costume.
A drummer fish with fins that tap,
Keeps the beat of nature's map.

Kelp forests sway, a line dance step,
While plankton giggle and misstep.
Oysters snicker, pearl by pearl,
Creating an underwater whirl!

With every pulse, the sea's alive,
Where shiny shells rock and jive.
The sea swans waddle, oh so sweet,
Their flippers move to the happy beat.

So tune your hearts to the great expanse,
Join the fish in the ocean's dance.
With rhythmic echoes, joy's not far,
The ocean glitters like a star!

The Forgotten Choir of the Abyss

In the deep, they sing with glee,
A fish on a mic, what a sight to see!
Gurgling tunes with a bubble beat,
While crabs clap along with their little feet.

Sea cucumbers hum out of tune,
Rays of sunlight make them groove 'til noon.
The starfish just sways, all laid back,
Dreaming of someday leading the pack.

Blowfish puffing up in pride,
As dolphins dance with their keen glide.
Octopus with a flair for style,
Twisting and turning, all in a while.

Yet the jellyfish floats, all aloof,
Wondering if it'll lead the next hoof.
In the abyss, laughter stays,
In the choir's depths, joyous waves.

Waves of Ancient Wisdom

Old turtles swim with tales so grand,
Sharing secrets across the sand.
With a wink and a nod, they cast their line,
While the seahorses sip on seaweed wine.

A clam opens wide, to share a joke,
While crabs do a shuffle, no need to poke.
The barnacles cling and laugh with might,
At the antics of fish in the moon's soft light.

Fish with glasses, reading the tide,
Trying to catch up, they're far behind.
But the rockfish grins, with knowledge vast,
As he swims to the future, forgetting the past.

With chorus of bubbles, wisdom flows,
In the waves where the laughter grows.
A comedic realm beneath the spray,
Where creatures chuckle at life's ballet.

Whispers from the Dark Blue

In the silent depths where shadows swing,
An anglerfish makes the dark heart sing.
With a flicker of light, it sways and glows,
While clownfish burst to steal the show!

A flounder rolls eyes, playing hard to see,
Pretending to nap like it's all just debris.
The sea serpent chuckles from behind a rock,
While mermaids giggle at their fishy flock.

Octopus over here playing peek-a-boo,
Changing colors, what a clever crew!
The dolphins jump, making dreams take flight,
Singing to stars with pure delight.

With whispers of laughter, the deep does hum,
Fish with a flair, always on the run.
In the dark blue sea, joy does persist,
As they dance along with a splash and a twist.

Harmonies in the Coral Kingdom

Oh, the coral holds a lively feast,
Where every creature comes, to say the least.
With a parrotfish strumming on a reef guitar,
And groupers tapping toes, oh what a bazaar!

Clownfish in a jester's hat,
Eel on a drum, imagine that!
A sea turtle serenades with a slow tune,
While the rest of the crew gets loose by moon.

A shrimp plays the spoons, oh what a scene,
Twirling and whirling, like a dance machine.
The purple urchins sway with style,
Cheering each fish, oh stay for a while!

Harmony sings in bright coral hues,
With laughter echoing through ocean views.
In this kingdom of colors, joy swims free,
A whimsical world, a vibrant jubilee.

The Unseen Choir of the Ocean's Heart

Bubbles burst, notes do flow,
Fish in tuxedos put on a show.
A dolphin trips over its own fin,
They laugh in waves, let the fun begin!

Starfish are clapping, what a surprise,
As sea cucumbers juggle before our eyes.
An octopus plays the violin,
While crabs cheer on, their pinchers in spin!

Turtles tap dance in a floating ball,
Shimmering scales reflect the call.
The sea floor's the stage, the tide's the beat,
In the ocean's palace, they can't be beat!

From sunlit shallows to depths unknown,
The rhythm of laughter is brightly sown.
In this concert of glee, it's plain to see,
That underwater antics make all fish agree!

Songs of the Submerged Realm

Coral can't help but shimmy and sway,
As seahorses trot in a quirky ballet.
Anemones giggle, tickled by the tide,
Chasing the bubbles, they twist with pride.

Mantis shrimp burst forth with a pop!
Singing high notes that never drop.
Clownfish chuckle, their colors ablaze,
In underwater mischief, they spend their days.

Lobsters clap claws to a jazzy tune,
Blowing bubbles under a glowing moon.
A group of squid starts to spin and glide,
In synchronized moves, they take a ride!

The ocean's a stage where laughter thrives,
Every creature's dance just brightens lives.
With fins and flippers that flap and fly,
The deep's a comedy where all can sigh!

Murmurs of Marine Mysteries

In kelp forests where shadows play,
Eels pop up to join the fray.
A blowfish blows up for a giggly jest,
While jellyfish drift in their glittery vest.

Scallops sing softly, a gentle hum,
Crabs pull pranks, then rush to run.
The sea urchins chuckle, prickly and bright,
As fish start their karaoke night!

A whale in the distance, with glee it lingers,
Slapping the water with happy flippers.
As waves hold the laughter, it's deep and wide,
Even the currents can't help but glide!

In this realm of chatter, a grand disguise,
Seashells whisper sweet lullabies.
The inexplicable joys surfacing bold,
Make every dive a story told!

Rhythms of the Blue Abyss

In the depths where few dare to roam,
Sea creatures jive happily at home.
A lost shoe bobs, perfect for a dance,
As fish twirl around in a humorous prance.

Gentle waves tickle a sleeping ray,
While snappy lobsters decide to play.
A walrus unveils its juggling act,
As starry-eyed fish offer up their pact.

With currents like trumpets, they sway with zest,
In the grand ocean party, they're truly blessed.
Tangled in laughter, they whizz and they whoosh,
Underwater circus, it's an endless swoosh!

So if you dive deep and hear a good cheer,
Know that the ocean's jokes are near.
In this aquatic frenzy, wild and free,
Even the beasts share a laugh with glee!

Lullabies of the Abyss

In the deep where creatures twirl,
A fish hums softly, giving a whirl.
Octopuses dance in pajamas bright,
Singing to crabs in the pale moonlight.

Starfish clap with limbs like hands,
While whales juggle shells in bands.
A seahorse strums on a coral guitar,
Making tunes that echo far.

Turtles tap to the beat of the tide,
As dolphins leap and glide with pride.
The anglerfish winks with a glowing grin,
Telling jokes under waves with a spin.

So if you listen with curious ears,
You'll hear the laughter beneath the spheres.
A symphony of glee beneath the foam,
In the depths, they've all found a home.

Harmonics of the Ocean's Heart

Bubbling bass from a clam's abode,
Makes for a quirky, underwater road.
The sea cucumbers shake with delight,
Giggling as they wiggle out of sight.

With every gush and bubbling sound,
A chorus of sea life spins around.
The flounder flails in a slapstick way,
While shrimp try to dance, they trip and sway.

Clownfish chuckle, dressed in stripes,
Telling tall tales of floating gripes.
Jellyfish float with jelly-like grace,
Wobbling along in a silly embrace.

Each melody radiates laughter's charm,
As creatures swirl without a qualm.
In a world beneath the watery art,
The ocean hums from its very heart.

Voices Beneath the Waves

In the briny deep, bubbles pop and soar,
Fish are gossiping, oh, what a roar!
The seahorse whispers tales of fright,
As a crab tells jokes that tickle the night.

Anemones sway, their arms up high,
To the rhythm of murmurs that catch the eye.
Squid throw a party with ink in the pool,
But one slips and splashes, what a fool!

Lobsters debate with a crustacean's flair,
One can't get a word in with the others' glare.
They bubble and curse as they scuttle around,
A raucous assembly in frothy sound.

Octopus poets weave stories of fun,
While the fish tap their fins, one by one.
Beneath the blue, there's laughter and cheer,
In the chorus of glee, let's give a cheer!

Tides of Ancient Serenades

Old shells spin tales of yesteryear,
As dolphins pop popcorn for circles near.
A mermaid giggles, her scales aglow,
Playing hide and seek with a confident blow.

Giant squids have writing contests to see,
Who can ink the silliest poetry.
A crab battles a clam for the best line,
As laughter bounces through brine with shine.

Bubbles rise high with secrets to tell,
Eel's puns are the best—can't you tell?
The seaweed swirls, swaying in goofy dance,
Inviting all fish for a whimsical prance.

With tides weaving tales of joy and delight,
The ocean sings softly into the night.
So dive deep and join, let your spirit be free,
In the laughter of waves, you'll find glee!

A Symphony of Lost Souls

In the deep where shadows play,
Fish dance along in a ballet.
A clam hums a tune so bright,
While crabs wink in the pale moonlight.

A turtle's giggle echoes quite loud,
As dolphins form a wiggly crowd.
They trade little jokes in their own way,
Making the squid blush with dismay.

With a hiccup, an octopus rolls,
And seaweed sways, and it strolls.
The anemones sway with glee,
"Is this concert just for me?"

Bubbles rise, they pop and burst,
As pencils and paper fish just thirst.
They scribble tales of a silly night,
In the ocean's own slapstick light.

Reverberations Beneath the Surface

Crabs tap dance on the ocean bed,
With clam shells clapping, full of dread.
A jellyfish wears a bowler hat,
While seahorses jokingly spat.

An eel tells tales of his great love,
To a starfish snoozing under the cove.
They chuckle at the tides' silly charm,
While barnacles sway, clinging with warm.

"Why did the fish blush?" the shark asks,
"Because it saw the surfboard's masks!"
And laughter bubbles up from the sand,
As the seafloor hosts a slapstick band.

With each splash, the night unfolds,
As the sea throws bubbles of stories told.
The deep is filled with a lively cheer,
Where every wave tickles an ear.

Nautical Echoes in Silence

Underneath the bright moon's gleam,
A pufferfish crafts a silly dream.
With blowfish giggles that bounce around,
The laughter swirls, a joyous sound.

Starfish play cards with a wink and a grin,
While rocks make bets and join in.
A mermaid snorts while holding her drink,
As the seaweed sways and starts to think.

Grouper in shades places a bet,
On who'll be the silliest, don't forget!
With conch shells whispering secrets so fine,
And sea cucumbers giggling all in line.

So in this blue where fish take flight,
The ocean's humor dances in light.
With currents that tickle and frolic about,
It's a splashy affair, there's never a doubt.

Pulses of the Oceanic Heart

Beats like a drum in the ocean grasp,
As fish keep time to a silvery rasp.
With a hippo in goggles doing a dive,
And a mermaid proclaiming, "We're alive!"

Turtles strut wearing glasses so round,
Like bowler hats upon the ground.
They pose for selfies with glittery fish,
While laughing at each outlandish wish.

Shrimps dart like arrows on a spree,
As they challenge the jellyfish to a spree.
With bubbles that giggle and play in the tide,
The ocean's heartbeats, a whimsical ride.

So listen in close to the aquatic art,
As laughter entwines with each oceanic heart.
With waves that swirl their comedic flair,
Underwater shenanigans fill the air.

Echoes from the Aquatic Wilderness

In the depths, a fish does dance,
With a wiggle and a silly prance.
He sings to the tuna, a comical tune,
While a crab joins in with a clumsy croon.

A dolphin flips and tries to glide,
But slips on kelp and takes a ride.
The octopus chuckles, ink in the air,
As he tickles a turtle with a jellyfish scare.

A seal dons a hat made of seaweed,
Proclaims he's a captain, oh yes indeed!
With a laugh and a bark, he sails around,
Causing a splash that's quite profound.

Bubbles giggle as they rise with glee,
Making melodies 'neath the big blue sea.
All creatures join in, a party divine,
In the underwater realm, where whimsy does shine.

The Melodrama of Silent Waters

Deep in the sea, where the quiet bides,
A fish tries to sing, but the sound just hides.
He clears his throat, a heroic jest,
But all that comes out is a gurgly quest.

Anemones sway, with dramatic flair,
As they roll their tentacles, styling with care.
A clam on the side lets out a huge yawn,
Reacting to drama like it's just gone dawn.

A seahorse attempts a tragic ballet,
But tangles his tail, and oh, what a display!
His partner, a jelly, just jiggly groans,
While passing starfish roll their many stone bones.

With laughter and chaos, the ocean erupts,
As the fish tries again, but the beat it corrupts.
The silence is broken, the fish is now bold,
With a song full of giggles, it's a sight to behold.

Chant of the Forgotten Waves

At twilight's edge, the tides come in,
With echoes of laughter, and splashes of fin.
A fish with a mustache plays the flute,
As shrimp in a conga dance, oh how cute!

An old turtle recalls the jokes of the sea,
With puns about pearls that are just for thee.
He winks at the others, what a wise guy,
As sea urchins chuckle, and bubbles comply.

The clam takes a bow, to the phosphor night,
While glowing plankton put up their light.
They twinkle and shimmer, a glittery show,
As seaweed sway to the tunes down below.

With each little wave, the fun multiplies,
As creatures enchant with their humorous tries.
In the depths of the blue, their laughter takes flight,
In a watery concert under the moonlight.

The Silent Symphony of Marine Depths

In hush of the deep, the critters conspire,
To create a performance that won't soon expire.
A hermit crab tries to strut in a shell,
But slips on a sandbank and tumbles so well.

Clownfish giggle in colors so bright,
As they swim through the coral, a comedic sight.
They throw in some quips, with each little flip,
While the sea cucumber just takes a sip.

An eel in disguise, a wiggly prankster,
Shocks a starfish with surprise, what a trickster!
They all join together, this motley crew,
In a silly ballet, oh the hullabaloo!

In the secretive calm, where the light starts to fade,
A symphony stirs, a jubilous parade.
Songs of the underwater, laughter entwined,
In the silent depths where joy is unconfined.

The Secret Chords of the Deep

In the deep blue, fish do dance,
With gills that gleam, they take a chance.
Bubbles burst like laughter loud,
Underwater, it's quite a crowd.

Tones so goofy, echoes bounce,
Even crabs try to sing and flounce.
Octopus joins with eight long arms,
Swirling notes, the ocean charms.

A dolphin snickers, flips around,
Making waves, it's quite profound.
Heard the turtles hum along,
In the currents, they belong.

As seaweed sways, the rhythm flows,
Clams clap shells, as humor grows.
In this choir of liquid cheer,
Every fish has a chance to steer.

Songs from the Twilight Depths

In twilight realms where shadows play,
Creatures chant the night away.
Anemones with voices sweet,
Tickle fish that can't be beat.

A sardine faint, "I think I'm lost,"
A seahorse cheers, "Just have a toss!"
With fins like feathers, krill will jive,
Grooving like it's 9-to-5.

Giant squids in a bubble bath,
Extravagant, they love themath!
They tickle rays with their long limbs,
While jellyfish do cheeky whims.

Mirthful echoes greet the night,
As fishy friends share pure delight.
The currents carry gentle grins,
In deep waters, everyone wins.

Mysterious Calls of the Abyss

In darkened depths where secrets weave,
A catfish whispers, "Don't you grieve."
With gurgling giggles, make a splash,
Surprise the eel, make a dash!

Amidst the reefs, a clam declares,
"Who needs a voice? I'm full of flares!"
Starfish giggle with arms so wide,
As pufferfish take the silly ride.

The anglerfish with lantern bright,
Jests, "Follow me, it's quite a sight!"
In shadows low, the jokes go round,
Bubbles form in laughter sounds.

Seahorses play a wiggly game,
These gentle souls aren't much to blame.
The abyss crackles with whimsy's light,
Mysterious joys that take to flight.

Lyrical Legends of the Brine

In legend's weave beneath the tide,
Fish tell stories with goofy pride.
A tuna spins yarns; oh, what a tale,
Of flounders dancing, quite frail!

With fins aflutter, the group convenes,
Triggerfish play, creating scenes.
A starry night made of fishy lore,
Elaborate tales from ocean's floor.

The sea cucumber, with wobbly poise,
Shares how he outsmarted a swarm of noise.
And every kraken now shakes with laughter,
Recalling their stunts and goofy after.

In briny depths where quirks align,
Creativity flows; they intertwine.
In their watery realm, they find delight,
Life's a giggle in the moonlit night.

Ballads of the Beneath

Bubbles rise with glee, oh dear,
A fish in a tux, what a sight here!
He twirls and he swirls, so full of flair,
Dancing with seaweed, without a care!

A crab starts to tap, he's got some moves,
While jellyfish jive, and the sea turtle grooves.
They'll hold a grand ball in the deep blue sea,
With clams as the judges, oh who will it be?

The octopus plays like a polka star,
His tentacles flailing, they're never too far.
A dolphin jumps in, he's a real party guy,
Flipping and splashing, with a wink of an eye!

So hear the laughter, echoing free,
In the underwater disco, what a spree!
With bubbles and giggles, let the rhythm sway,
In the depths of the ocean, it's a wild day!

Rhythms of the Forgotten Depths

At the bottom of the sea, life's a reel,
Goldfish in sunglasses, spinning their wheel.
A clownfish whispers a joke to a shrimp,
And all of the crabs chime in with a wimp!

Anemones sway with the tunes in the tide,
Waving their arms, they're a colorful guide.
They've got the bass, oh, it's quite a show,
Even the sea stars join in the flow!

With sea cucumbers acting all cool,
Forming a line like they're going to school.
A mermaid grins, flipping her hair,
"Join us down here, for we've got flair!"

Echoes of laughter fill the blue halls,
As a big, old turtle just takes fun falls.
With rhythms and giggles, they dance on the floor,
In the forgotten depths, there's always more!

Tides of Ancient Harmony

Once in the deep, where the fishes chatter,
A starfish claimed fame, but it really was flatter.
With a shell on his head, he strutted his stuff,
"Shall we dance now, or is that too tough?"

The dolphins are laughing, oh what a sight,
While seahorses spin, taking flight.
They gather around for a grand ol' time,
To the rhythm of waves, in perfect rhyme!

A coral reef hosted, a grand finball,
With sea bass as bouncers, they stood tall.
Clams dropped the beat, with pearls on display,
And anemones lit up the lively way!

From the depths of the blue, to the shimmering top,
The tides sway and swirl, they never will stop.
So join in the fun, in this magical sea,
Where ancient harmony makes you feel free!

The Lullaby of Sea Giants

In the deep where giants roam,
A whale belches bubbles, far from home.
With a wiggle and giggle, he sings out loud,
Making the narwhals form a proud crowd!

The sharks take a nap, snoring all around,
While a stingray glides, without a sound.
"Shh!" whispers a crab, "Keep it all cool,"
As the octopus dreams, of one day in school!

The sea turtle snores, what a funny tune,
While a fish plays the fiddle beneath the moon.
Each melody floats, through the surf's gentle sway,
"Join in, my friends, let's dance and play!"

So laugh and hum, with the creatures nearby,
Under the stars, where the big fishes lie.
In this lullaby realm, so funny and bright,
The sea giants giggle, all through the night!

Enchanted Echoes in the Sea's Embrace

Bubbles rise with sounds so clear,
Fish gather close, they wish to hear.
A crab starts to dance, with grace and flair,
While a seahorse giggles in the salty air.

Starfish clap in their own slow way,
Clownfish laugh at the octopus play.
Turtles nod to the funny beat,
As dolphins dance on their little feet.

A clam sings low, but he's a bit shy,
While jellyfish float on by, oh my!
Sardines twirl in a silvery flash,
Joining the fun in a bubbly splash.

In this ocean where laughter reigns,
Every creature knows the playful strains.
So dive in deep, let joy abound,
In the water's waltz, good vibes are found!

Voices of the Luminous Abyss

In the depths where giggles bloom,
An anglerfish flashes in fancy costume.
A pufferfish pops with a comical sigh,
While sea cucumbers trundle by.

The coral sings with a hissing sound,
As anemones sway all around.
Shrimp play tag, they're in on the fun,
It's a party under the bright, warm sun.

A narwhal winks with a knowing smile,
As sea turtles take a swim in style.
The ocean's giggles never cease,
As every creature finds their peace.

With colors bright and jokes to share,
The ocean's whispers fill the air.
So join the dance, let laughter swell,
In the watery depths, all is well!

The Enigma of Ocean Melodies

Beneath the waves, the tunes arise,
With quirky notes that wiggle and surprise.
A flounder slips in a rhythmic slide,
As barnacles laugh, they can't hide their pride.

A shrimp plays drums on a clam's cool shell,
While a porpoise hums, ringing the bell.
Shimmery fish form a chorus line,
In the wet world where everyone shines.

Crabs tap dance, oh what a sight!
In this underwater cosmic night.
A stingray glides with flair and charm,
As the sea whispers jokes, wrapped in calm.

Every splash carries a playful tune,
A jester's show by the light of the moon.
So come take a dip, let laughter flow,
In this ocean of sounds where giggles grow!

An Underwater Reverie

In the depths where chuckles loom,
Grouchy grouper finds his groove.
With a twist and flip, he gets it right,
While clownfish laugh with all their might.

The seahorses waltz with whimsical grace,
As a moray eel makes a funny face.
The bubbles burst in a giddy spree,
While starfish hang out for tea.

A squishy blob sings a silly tune,
To the beat of waves beneath the moon.
A school of fish forms a magic show,
As laughter muffled calls, "Oh no!"

Join the frolic, don't be shy,
In this wet world where giggles fly.
So wiggle and splash, let spirits soar,
For in this sea, there's always more!

Voices of the Deepening Water

In the deep, they chatter, oh what a sound,
Fish wear their headphones, grooving around.
Crabs groove to bass while octopus plays,
Turtles just dance in a bubbly haze.

Seahorses giggle as they twirl and glide,
Starfish join in, they can't hide their pride.
With bubbles like beats, they all sing along,
A raucous parade, in the sea they belong.

Nemo's got rhythm, he's got quite a beat,
Clams do the conga, who knew they had feet?
The ocean's a party, a splashy delight,
Where laughter and bubbles last into the night.

So next time you swim, take a moment to hear,
The underwater jokers that spread so much cheer.
With gags and a splash, it's a silly affair,
In the depths of the ocean, there's magic everywhere.

Harmonies Lost to the Sea

Bubbles are popping like popcorn in air,
Fish are all singing, without any care.
A dolphin's a clown with a punchline or two,
His jokes are a hit, they'll leave you askew.

Crabby Bob's bragging, he caught a big wave,
While sea turtles plot how to misbehave.
The eels do a jig, they wriggle and squirm,
In this watery world, good luck with the term.

A mermaid's lost notes got tangled in seaweed,
Her voice like a kazoo, can't quite take the lead.
Stingrays are snickering, it's all in good fun,
As they glide through the blues, under the sun.

The ocean's a stage without any fear,
With creatures performing, oh, my, what a cheer!
So if you hear giggles beneath the salt deep,
Join in on the laughter, don't you dare keep.

Mystery in the Stillness

In quiet corners where shadows reside,
The sea critters gather, there's no need to hide.
A clam whispers secrets, stories untold,
While fish play charades in shimmering gold.

Anemones giggle as currents flow past,
With a wave and a wink, they're having a blast.
A jellyfish floats by, with style and cheer,
In this silent ballet, no one's in fear.

Octopus sits thinking, his tentacles crossed,
Wondering what happened to his friend, the lost.
With laughter still lingering, they search high and low,
For the treasures of laughter that help friendships grow.

So when silence is golden in the depths of the sea,
Remember, it's filled with sweet melody.
Mysteries swirl but all's well and bright,
In the stillness, there's magic, a heartwarming sight.

Chants from the Ocean Floor

Beneath the blue, there's a whispering tale,
Of fish with big dreams that never set sail.
They giggle at shadows, they clown all about,
The wise old turtle has seen it, no doubt.

Corals are gossiping, weaving their threads,
While crabs tell tall tales of their juicy spreads.
An anglerfish grins with his light bulb so bright,
"I'm the ultimate catch, don't turn out the light!"

Guppies play tag in a swirling delight,
As eels aim to trip them, what a silly sight!
With laughter erupting in gurgles and splashes,
The sea floor's alive with their jigs and their dashes.

So next time you wander through waves all around,
Know there's humor in depths where the sillies abound.
The ocean's not quiet; it chuckles and plays,
A haven of giggles in countless strange ways.

www.ingramcontent.com/pod-product-compliance
Lightning Source LLC
Chambersburg PA
CBHW060139230426
43661CB00003B/482